The Quantum Mindset

The Quantum Mindset

Matthew Petchinsky

1

The Quantum Mindset: Think Like a Billionaire

By: Matthew Petchinsky

Introduction: The Power of Quantum Thinking

The human mind is one of the most powerful forces in existence. It has the capacity to dream, create, and reshape reality itself. Yet, most people operate under a fixed, linear mindset—one bound by limitations, scarcity, and outdated models of success. The Quantum Mindset is different. It is the key to unlocking boundless opportunities, limitless wealth, and a life of extraordinary possibilities.

At its core, the Quantum Mindset is about shifting from traditional, mechanical ways of thinking to a dynamic, expansive way of perceiving the world—one that mirrors the principles of quantum physics. It is the mindset of billionaires, visionaries, and world-changers who understand that success is not simply about hard work or luck, but about harnessing the very fabric of reality to create the life they desire.

What Is Quantum Thinking?

Quantum thinking is not just about intelligence or logic; it's about perception, adaptability, and understanding the infinite potential within every moment. It's about seeing beyond conventional limits and tapping into a world of probabilities where you are the master of your destiny.

Traditional thinking is linear: if you take action A, you will get result B. Quantum thinking, on the other hand, acknowledges that multiple possibilities exist at once, and your ability to influence reality is far greater than you've been led to believe. It is a fusion of science, philosophy, and wealth consciousness—an approach that the world's most successful individuals intuitively grasp.

Billionaires like Elon Musk, Jeff Bezos, and Warren Buffett don't just follow a straight path to success. They leverage an expansive, multidimensional perspective that allows them to identify unseen opportunities, take bold risks, and create innovative solutions where others see obstacles. They embrace uncertainty, use intuition, and harness the power of their thoughts to manifest their goals.

The Science Behind the Quantum Mindset

Quantum physics teaches us that reality is not as fixed as we once believed. Subatomic particles exist in multiple states simultaneously until observed—a phenomenon known as superposition. This principle extends to life and success as well. Every moment holds infinite potential outcomes, and your focus and beliefs determine which reality you step into.

Moreover, quantum entanglement shows that everything in the universe is interconnected. Your thoughts, emotions, and actions send out energetic signals that influence the reality around you. This is why people who think in terms of abundance tend to attract more wealth, and why those who constantly focus on scarcity often remain stuck in a cycle of lack.

Understanding these principles is the first step to mastering the Quantum Mindset. By shifting the way you think, speak, and act, you begin to align yourself with the frequency of success and opportunity.

Breaking Free from the Old Paradigm

Most people are trapped in a limited, deterministic way of thinking—one shaped by society, upbringing, and outdated beliefs. They believe success is reserved for the privileged, that money is hard to come by, or that they must follow a traditional career path to achieve financial freedom. This is a scarcity-based mindset, and it is the very thing keeping them from unlocking their true potential.

The Quantum Mindset teaches you to break free from these limitations. Instead of seeing money as something that requires endless struggle, you begin to view it as an energy—something that flows to those who understand how to attract and direct it. Instead of fearing uncertainty, you learn to embrace it as a field of endless opportunities. Instead of believing in competition, you adopt a mindset of limitless creation.

Thinking Like a Billionaire

Billionaires don't just think differently; they operate in an entirely different paradigm. They understand that wealth is created from ideas, vision, and execution—not from following the same path as everyone else. They don't react to circumstances; they create them. They see the world as malleable, shaped by their thoughts, actions, and beliefs.

To adopt the Quantum Mindset, you must train yourself to think like a billionaire. This means:

- **Expanding your perception of possibility** – The world is not as rigid as it seems. The wealth and success you desire already exist; you simply need to align yourself with it.
- **Making bold, decisive moves** – Wealth is not built through hesitation. Those who succeed are willing to act with certainty, even in the face of uncertainty.
- **Embracing failure as part of success** – Quantum thinking acknowledges that setbacks are not roadblocks, but course corrections leading to greater opportunities.
- **Focusing on solutions, not problems** – While the average person sees obstacles, billionaires see stepping stones to innovation and growth.
- **Cultivating an abundance mindset** – The Quantum Mindset recognizes that there is no limit to wealth, success, or opportunity. The more you create, the more you attract.

The Journey Ahead

This book will serve as your guide to developing the Quantum Mindset—teaching you how to think, act, and operate like a billionaire. Each chapter will reveal the secrets of quantum thinking, breaking down the principles of success, wealth attraction, and limitless potential.

By the time you finish reading, you will no longer see the world in the same way. You will understand that your mind holds the power to shape your reality. You will no longer be a passive observer of life—you will be an active creator.

Prepare to unlock a new dimension of thinking. Prepare to step into your quantum power.

Your journey to thinking like a billionaire begins now.

Chapter 1: The Science Behind Success – Why Billionaires Think Differently

Success is not an accident, nor is it reserved for the privileged few. The world's wealthiest and most influential individuals operate on a different level—not because of luck or inherited wealth, but because of their ability to think in a way that most people do not. They leverage the power of their mind, energy, and decision-making process to create opportunities, rather than waiting for them to appear.

This chapter will explore the science behind success and how billionaires think differently, not just in their actions but in their fundamental understanding of reality. From neuroscience to quantum physics, we will break down the key principles that set them apart.

The Billionaire Brain: How the Mind Shapes Reality

It's no secret that our thoughts shape our reality. Science has proven that the way we think affects our brain structure, decision-making processes, and ultimately, our success. The human brain is wired for survival, meaning most people think in ways that prioritize safety, predictability, and comfort. However, billionaires do not operate from this default mindset. Instead, they have trained their brains to embrace risk, think expansively, and recognize opportunities where others see obstacles.

Neuroplasticity: Rewiring the Brain for Success

Neuroplasticity refers to the brain's ability to adapt and change throughout life. This means that the way you think is not fixed—it can be reshaped to align with success. Studies in neuroscience have shown that successful people develop mental habits that strengthen neural pathways associated with confidence, resilience, and problem-solving.

Billionaires train their brains to:

- **See opportunity where others see failure** – Instead of focusing on losses, they focus on learning and adjusting strategies.
- **Think in terms of abundance, not scarcity** – They believe that wealth and success are limitless, rather than finite resources.
- **Act decisively and take calculated risks** – They make bold moves without fear of failure, understanding that action creates momentum.

One example is **Elon Musk**, who constantly pushes the boundaries of what is possible in space travel, artificial intelligence, and energy solutions. His brain is wired to solve massive problems rather than dwell on limitations.

The Reticular Activating System: Filtering Success

The **Reticular Activating System (RAS)** is a small network of neurons in the brainstem responsible for filtering information. Every day, we are bombarded with millions of pieces of data, but the RAS decides what is important based on our beliefs and focus.

Billionaires program their RAS to seek opportunities. They condition their minds to recognize wealth-building possibilities, investment trends, and profitable ventures, even in situations where others see nothing. If you constantly focus on success, your RAS will filter out distractions and bring opportunities into your awareness.

This is why affirmations, visualization, and goal setting are powerful tools. They train your brain to identify pathways to wealth that were previously invisible to you.

Quantum Thinking: How Billionaires Use Reality to Their Advantage

Beyond neuroscience, quantum physics offers profound insights into how successful individuals think. Unlike classical physics, which views reality as fixed and deterministic, quantum physics suggests that reality is fluid and shaped by the observer.

The Observer Effect: Reality Responds to Focus

Quantum experiments have proven that subatomic particles exist in multiple states until observed—a phenomenon known as the **Observer Effect**. This means that reality shifts based on observation, intention, and energy.

Billionaires intuitively understand this principle. They don't wait for reality to dictate their future—they dictate reality. They believe in their success so deeply that they create the conditions for it to manifest. This is why **visionary entrepreneurs** like Steve Jobs were able to build empires based on ideas that seemed impossible at the time.

Quantum Superposition: Holding Multiple Possibilities

Unlike traditional thinkers who see life in black and white (success or failure, wealth or poverty), billionaires think in **quantum superposition**, meaning they hold multiple possibilities at once.

For example:

- Instead of thinking, *Will this business idea succeed or fail?*, they ask, *How can I make this business succeed under multiple conditions?*
- Instead of asking, *Can I become wealthy or not?*, they ask, *What pathways to wealth am I currently overlooking?*

This mindset allows them to navigate uncertainty and make bold moves without hesitation. They don't get paralyzed by fear or binary thinking—they see infinite options and act accordingly.

The Psychology of Billionaires: Key Traits That Separate Them from the Average Thinker

Billionaires are not just rich in money; they are rich in **thought patterns and behaviors** that create financial abundance. Their way of thinking is fundamentally different from the average person's.

1. They Think Long-Term

Most people operate on short-term gratification. Billionaires, however, play the long game. They make investments, build businesses, and cultivate networks that may not pay off for years but will eventually lead to massive returns.

Example:

- **Jeff Bezos** started Amazon in his garage and didn't turn a profit for years. He prioritized long-term dominance over short-term earnings, eventually creating one of the most valuable companies in the world.

2. They Take Risks, but Not Recklessly

Risk-taking is a fundamental trait of billionaires, but they take **calculated risks** based on research, intuition, and strategy. They understand that without risk, there is no growth.

Example:

- **Elon Musk** risked nearly all his fortune on Tesla and SpaceX, knowing that innovation required bold action. He was willing to fail multiple times because he believed in the long-term vision.

3. They Control Their Time

Time is the most valuable asset billionaires have. They do not trade time for money—they make money work for them. They delegate, automate, and focus only on high-impact activities.

Example:

- **Warren Buffett** spends the majority of his time reading and thinking, rather than engaging in busywork. He understands that deep thinking leads to better investment decisions.

4. They Understand the Power of Networks

Success is not built in isolation. Billionaires surround themselves with other high-level thinkers, forming powerful networks that create new opportunities. They understand that relationships are currency.

Example:

- **Richard Branson** built Virgin Group by forming strategic partnerships and leveraging relationships to enter new industries.

5. They Stay Adaptable and Innovative

Billionaires are not rigid in their thinking. They **embrace change** and pivot when necessary. They stay ahead of trends and position themselves to capitalize on new markets.

Example:

- **Mark Zuckerberg** adapted Facebook's business model multiple times, evolving it from a social network into a global tech giant with multiple revenue streams.

Conclusion: The Quantum Shift in Thinking

Success is not just about what you do—it's about how you **think**. The science behind success reveals that billionaires operate from a different mental paradigm—one rooted in **neuroscience, quantum physics, and psychology**.

If you want to think like a billionaire, you must:

◈ **Rewire your brain for success** through neuroplasticity and focus.
◈ **Train your RAS to recognize wealth-building opportunities.**
◈ **Adopt quantum thinking**—seeing multiple possibilities instead of limits.
◈ **Play the long game, take calculated risks, and control your time.**
◈ **Surround yourself with high-level thinkers and embrace adaptability.**

The shift from **linear thinking to quantum thinking** is the key to unlocking unlimited success.

Your journey to billionaire thinking has just begun. ◈

Chapter 2: Quantum Wealth – The Art of Attracting Unlimited Money

Money is not just paper or numbers in a bank account—it is energy. The difference between those who struggle financially and those who accumulate massive wealth lies in their **mindset, subconscious programming, and ability to harness the power of quantum wealth attraction**.

Billionaires and financially successful individuals do not chase money—they **attract it**. They understand that wealth is an energetic frequency, and by aligning their thoughts, beliefs, and actions with financial abundance, they create unlimited opportunities.

In this chapter, we will explore the principles of **Quantum Wealth**, breaking down how to cultivate an unstoppable wealth mindset and program your subconscious to attract financial abundance.

The Quantum Wealth Formula: How Money is Attracted, Not Pursued

Traditional financial advice teaches people to **work hard, save, and invest**—but if that were the only formula for wealth, then millions of hardworking people wouldn't be living paycheck to paycheck.

Quantum Wealth operates differently. It is based on the **energetic nature of money**, the laws of attraction, and the way successful people use their minds to generate prosperity effortlessly.

The Frequency of Money

Everything in the universe vibrates at a specific frequency—including money. When you operate from a **scarcity mindset**, focusing on debt, financial struggle, and lack, you **emit a low vibration that repels money**.

On the other hand, when you shift into **abundance consciousness**, you align yourself with the frequency of wealth, and money begins to flow effortlessly into your life.

Billionaires understand that money flows to those who:

- **Expect abundance as their natural state**
- **Think expansively and see opportunities everywhere**
- **Feel deserving of unlimited wealth**
- **Detach from scarcity-based fears and limitations**

To attract **Quantum Wealth**, you must first tune into the **money frequency** and remove any subconscious blocks preventing financial abundance from entering your life.

How to Cultivate an Unstoppable Wealth Mindset

Your mindset is your greatest asset or your biggest liability when it comes to wealth. A **wealth mindset** is the mental framework that allows money to flow effortlessly into your life, while a **poverty mindset** creates endless financial struggle.

Step 1: Identify and Reprogram Limiting Beliefs About Money

Most people are **subconsciously programmed** to repel wealth because of negative beliefs they absorbed from society, family, and past experiences.

Some of the most **common limiting beliefs** include:

◈ "Money is the root of all evil."

◈ "I have to work hard to make money."

◈ "Wealthy people are greedy or corrupt."

◈ "I am not lucky or privileged enough to be rich."

◈ "Making money is difficult."

These beliefs operate **beneath the surface of your conscious mind**, sabotaging your financial success. If you hold these beliefs, you will unconsciously **push money away** even when opportunities arise.

◈ **Solution: Rewire Your Subconscious with New Money Beliefs**

- **Money is a tool for freedom and impact.**
- **I attract wealth effortlessly because I align with abundance.**
- **The more money I receive, the more good I can do in the world.**
- **Opportunities to create wealth are limitless.**
- **Wealth flows to me in expected and unexpected ways.**

Repetition of these **affirmations** daily will **reprogram your subconscious** and shift your energy toward wealth attraction.

Step 2: Use the Power of Visualization to Magnetize Money

Your brain cannot tell the difference between a vividly imagined experience and reality. This is why visualization is a powerful tool for programming your mind for financial success.

How to visualize wealth effectively:

1. **Close your eyes and picture yourself already wealthy.** See the lifestyle, the bank account, the freedom.
2. **Feel the emotions of abundance.** What does it feel like to live without financial stress?
3. **Engage all senses.** Imagine holding a check with multiple zeros, driving your dream car, or walking through your luxury home.
4. **Do this daily for 5-10 minutes.** This trains your subconscious mind to accept wealth as a **natural state**.

Billionaires **see** their success before it happens. They mentally live in their future wealth **before** it manifests in reality.

Step 3: Align with Abundance by Eliminating Scarcity Thinking

Most people block financial success by obsessing over what they **lack**. Scarcity thinking includes:

- Worrying about bills
- Stressing over how much things cost
- Believing there is never enough money

Billionaires think the opposite way. Instead of **scarcity**, they focus on **creation, value, and opportunity**.

◈ **To align with abundance:**

◈ **Stop focusing on lack.** Shift your thoughts toward wealth and possibilities.

◈ **Practice gratitude for your current wealth.** Even if you have little, appreciate it. Gratitude attracts more.

◈ **Surround yourself with wealth-conscious people.** Energy is contagious—be around people who think big.

Programming Your Subconscious for Financial Abundance

The subconscious mind is responsible for **95% of your thoughts and behaviors**. If you are not wealthy yet, it is likely because your subconscious programming is **blocking** financial success.

Techniques to Reprogram Your Subconscious for Wealth:

1. Auto-Suggestion & Repetitive Affirmations

Speak wealth-based affirmations **daily** until they become your subconscious truth:

- "I am a money magnet."
- "Abundance flows effortlessly into my life."
- "I deserve unlimited financial success."

2. Subconscious Reprogramming Audios

Listen to **binaural beats** or **affirmation recordings** while sleeping to rewire your subconscious effortlessly.

3. Wealth Journaling

Write down **your financial goals and beliefs daily** as if they are already achieved:

- "I earn $100,000 per month with ease."
- "My investments grow exponentially every year."

4. Energy Clearing Techniques

Use **meditation, breathwork, or EFT tapping** to remove old money traumas and scarcity programming.

Billionaire Money Habits: How to Act as if You're Already Rich

Once your mindset is programmed for wealth, your **actions** must align. Billionaires **act** like billionaires before they become wealthy.

The Key Money Habits of Wealthy People:

⟐ **Invest in Self-Education.** Never stop learning about money, investing, and business.

⟐ **Make Decisions Based on Expansion, Not Fear.** Always ask, *Will this decision move me toward more abundance?*

⟐ **Create Multiple Streams of Income.** Wealthy people **never rely on one income source**.

⟐ **Give Generously.** The more you give, the more you receive.

⟐ **Think in Terms of Unlimited Possibilities.** Opportunities are infinite—never put limits on your financial growth.

Conclusion: Step Into Your Quantum Wealth Identity

Becoming financially successful is **not about working harder**—it's about **thinking differently**. Quantum Wealth is about shifting from **chasing money** to **attracting it effortlessly** through alignment, mindset, and energy.

⟐ **Reprogram your subconscious with powerful money beliefs.**

⟐ **Visualize and emotionally experience financial abundance before it manifests.**

⟐ **Eliminate scarcity thinking and replace it with an abundance mindset.**

⟐ **Develop billionaire money habits and make bold financial decisions.**

When you master the **Quantum Wealth Mindset**, money stops being a struggle and becomes a **natural byproduct of your energy and thinking**.

You are now on the path to thinking like a billionaire. ⯑

Chapter 3: Mind Over Matter – How Thoughts Reshape Reality

The difference between those who struggle financially and those who experience unlimited wealth is not intelligence, luck, or privilege—it is **how they think**. Every billionaire, entrepreneur, and financial titan understands a fundamental truth: **your thoughts create your reality.**

Wealth is not something you pursue—it is something you **attract by aligning your mind, energy, and actions with abundance**. This chapter will break down the science of **how thoughts shape reality** and teach you how to build **unstoppable momentum in your financial journey**, so wealth flows to you **continuously** and effortlessly.

The Science of Mind Over Matter: The Power of Thought

Most people believe reality is **fixed**—that they must work within the limitations of their circumstances. But quantum physics, neuroscience, and psychology prove that **your thoughts influence reality on a fundamental level.**

Every thought you think sends **a signal into the universe**, attracting experiences, people, and financial opportunities that align with your dominant mindset.

How Your Brain Shapes Reality

The **Reticular Activating System (RAS)** is a powerful filter in your brain that determines **what you notice in the world**. It is why, after buying a new car, you suddenly see the same model everywhere—it was always there, but now your brain is attuned to it.

The same principle applies to wealth:

- If you focus on **lack and struggle**, your brain will filter reality to reinforce those beliefs.

- If you train your mind to **expect wealth and opportunity**, your RAS will highlight chances to **make money, attract the right people, and recognize financial breakthroughs.**

Billionaires do not see the world the same way as the average person because **they have trained their brains to notice opportunities where others see obstacles.**

The Observer Effect: Reality Responds to Your Focus

Quantum physics has proven that reality does not exist in a fixed state—it changes based on **observation**. This is known as the **Observer Effect**, which states that subatomic particles exist in multiple states until observed.

What does this mean for wealth?

- If you focus on **lack, debt, and financial stress**, you reinforce that reality.
- If you shift your focus to **abundance, opportunities, and wealth**, reality reshapes itself to match that expectation.

Your **dominant thoughts act as a magnet**, pulling in experiences that confirm what you believe to be true.

◈ **Billionaires master the Observer Effect by training their minds to see only success, growth, and limitless opportunities.**

Building Unstoppable Momentum in Your Financial Journey

Momentum is the secret to **continuous wealth creation**. Just like a snowball rolling downhill, small actions build into **massive results** over time.

Here's how you can build **unstoppable momentum** so wealth **flows to you continuously**:

Step 1: Establish a Powerful Financial Identity

Your **identity** is the foundation of your wealth. If you see yourself as "just getting by" or "not good with money," your actions will reflect that identity.

◈ **Upgrade Your Financial Identity** by telling yourself:

- "I am a wealth creator."
- "I always attract financial opportunities."
- "Money flows to me effortlessly."

Once you shift your **identity**, your brain will automatically **seek ways to make that reality true.**

Step 2: Create Daily Wealth-Building Habits

Wealth is not created in a single moment—it is built through **consistent habits**. The secret of billionaires is that they develop **daily routines** that reinforce success.

◈ **Morning Wealth Visualization:** Spend 5 minutes visualizing your financial success as if it is already real.

◈ **Daily Income-Generating Activity:** Take **one small financial action** every day—invest, launch a project, network, or learn a new skill.

◈ **Nighttime Wealth Affirmations:** Before bed, repeat affirmations like, *"I am wealthy beyond measure,"* to reprogram your subconscious.

By stacking these **small habits daily**, your wealth momentum becomes unstoppable.

Step 3: Multiply Your Money Frequency with Action

Thoughts alone do not create wealth—**action is the amplifier**. Billionaires think in **expansion, not limitation**.

◈ **Action steps to multiply your financial momentum:**

◈ **Automate Your Income Streams** – Set up passive income so money flows without effort.

◈ **Leverage Other People's Skills** – Billionaires **delegate** instead of trying to do everything alone.

◈ **Invest, Don't Just Save** – Money **multiplies** when it is put into motion (real estate, stocks, digital products, businesses).

◈ **Network with High-Level Thinkers** – Surround yourself with people who **elevate** your thinking.

By **combining powerful thoughts with bold action**, you **activate the Quantum Wealth Cycle**—a self-sustaining system where money keeps flowing to you.

Overcoming Momentum Killers: The Hidden Blocks That Stop Wealth Flow

Just as momentum can build wealth, it can also **be destroyed by limiting beliefs and negative energy**. Here are the biggest momentum killers—and how to eliminate them:

◈ **Scarcity Mindset → ◈ Abundance Consciousness**

Instead of thinking, *"I never have enough money,"* shift to *"Wealth is unlimited, and I align with it."*

◈ **Fear of Failure → ◈ Embrace Risk as Growth**

Every billionaire **failed multiple times** before succeeding. View setbacks as **necessary stepping stones** to wealth.

◈ **Emotional Blocks → ◈ Cleanse Negative Money Energy**

If you feel **guilt, shame, or fear** around money, practice **money meditations, affirmations, and forgiveness exercises** to release financial resistance.

By **eliminating momentum killers**, you remove the brakes **holding your financial success back.**

The Quantum Flow State: Where Wealth Becomes Effortless

When your thoughts, emotions, and actions are **aligned with abundance**, you enter the **Quantum Flow State**—a powerful state where:

◈ Wealth opportunities appear **without force**.

◈ Financial success feels **effortless and natural**.

◈ You are in a continuous state of **expansion and attraction**.

Billionaires stay in the **Quantum Flow** by:

◈ **Following their intuition** – Trusting their gut when making financial moves.

◈ **Staying in a state of gratitude** – Feeling abundant **before** the money arrives.

◈ **Letting go of resistance** – Not stressing over HOW money will come, but trusting that it WILL.

Final Takeaways: How to Lock in Your Wealth Momentum Forever

By now, you understand that your **thoughts shape your financial reality**, and momentum is key to continuous wealth. To lock in this transformation:

◈ **Commit to a Wealth Identity** – Think like a billionaire NOW.

◈ **Stack Small Wealth Habits Daily** – Compound effect = massive success.

◈ **Eliminate Scarcity Thinking** – Shift to an **abundance-first mindset**.

◈ **Take Bold Action** – Move towards expansion, not fear.

◈ **Stay in the Quantum Flow** – Align thoughts, actions, and emotions with financial success.

When you train your mind to expect, attract, and multiply wealth, **money will no longer be something you chase—it will be something that continuously flows into your life.**

Your journey to unlimited wealth **has already begun.** ◈

Chapter 4: The Future of Wealth – AI, Technology, and Financial Evolution

We are living in the most transformative era of wealth creation in human history. The rise of artificial intelligence (AI), blockchain technology, and automation is reshaping how money flows, how businesses operate, and how wealth is accumulated. Those who understand this shift and position themselves correctly will become the next wave of billionaires.

But while technology is accelerating financial growth, **there are hidden universal laws of money** that the wealthy have always used to **magnetize riches with ease**. These laws operate beyond economic trends, technological advancements, or industry shifts. They are the **timeless principles that govern financial success**, and when combined with cutting-edge technology, they create an unstoppable force for wealth.

This chapter will uncover:

- The future of money and how AI is rewriting the rules of finance
- The hidden universal laws of money that the rich follow
- How to position yourself to take advantage of the next financial evolution

The Wealth Revolution: How AI and Technology Are Transforming Money

Technology has always played a role in financial growth, but we are now witnessing a **quantum leap in wealth acceleration**. AI and automation are making **businesses smarter, financial markets faster, and opportunities more abundant than ever before**.

1. AI is Creating a New Class of Billionaires

Artificial intelligence is no longer a futuristic concept—it is **the most powerful wealth-building tool available today**. The world's richest individuals and corporations are using AI to:

- **Predict market trends** and execute trades faster than any human
- **Automate businesses**, reducing costs while increasing revenue
- **Create new industries** that didn't exist a decade ago (AI-driven medicine, autonomous vehicles, AI-generated content)

Example:

Elon Musk, Mark Zuckerberg, and Jeff Bezos are all heavily invested in AI, positioning themselves at the forefront of this technological revolution. AI is **not just changing the game—it is creating entirely new financial playing fields.**

2. The Blockchain Economy: Decentralized Wealth Creation

Blockchain technology is redefining **how money is stored, transferred, and multiplied**. Cryptocurrency and decentralized finance (DeFi) have unlocked a **borderless, permissionless financial system** where anyone can build wealth without relying on traditional banks.

◈ **Why this matters:**

◈ Traditional banks are slow and restrictive; DeFi allows **instant global transactions**.

◈ NFTs (non-fungible tokens) and tokenized assets are **new forms of wealth storage**.

◈ The blockchain economy is creating **a financial system that runs without middlemen**.

Example:

Bitcoin started as an experiment but is now **a trillion-dollar asset class**. Those who understood its potential early became millionaires and billionaires **simply by being ahead of the curve**.

3. Automation and the Rise of Passive Income

Billionaires do not **trade time for money**—they build **self-sustaining income streams** that generate wealth continuously.

With AI and automation, **creating passive income is easier than ever**:

◈ AI-powered investing bots grow wealth 24/7.

◈ Automated e-commerce stores run **without human input**.

◈ AI-written content, art, and music create **royalties on autopilot**.

Lesson:

Those who learn **how to integrate AI, automation, and smart investing** into their wealth strategy will be ahead of 99% of the world.

The Hidden Universal Laws of Money the Wealthy Use to Magnetize Riches

While technology is changing **how** wealth is created, **the fundamental principles of wealth have remained the same for centuries**. The rich do not just work hard—they **apply hidden universal money laws** that allow them to attract and multiply wealth effortlessly.

These laws operate like **gravity**—whether you are aware of them or not, they govern your financial reality. Once you **align with these principles**, wealth becomes a **magnetic force** in your life.

1. The Law of Value Creation: Money Follows Impact

◈ **Money is a byproduct of value.** The more problems you solve, the more wealth you attract.

Wealthy individuals do not ask, *"How can I make money?"* They ask, **"How can I create massive value?"**

◈ **Example:**

Jeff Bezos became one of the richest men in history by solving a major problem—how to buy anything online with ease. Amazon's **value** created **trillions in wealth**.

◈ **Apply This Today:**

Find **one way to create value at scale**—start a business, offer a unique service, or automate a solution.

2. The Law of Wealth Alignment: Money Flows Where It's Welcomed

◈ **If you resent wealth, it will avoid you.**

Many people secretly believe money is:

◈ Evil or corrupt

◈ Hard to obtain

◈ Limited to the lucky few

These beliefs block wealth. The rich welcome money, respect it, and **expect it to flow freely into their lives**.

◈ **Example:**

Billionaires **think expansively**—instead of *"I can't afford this,"* they ask, **"How can I afford this?"** This shifts their mindset from limitation to creativity.

◈ **Apply This Today:**

Start saying **wealth-positive affirmations daily**:

◈ "I am a magnet for financial abundance."

◈ "Money flows to me easily and effortlessly."

◈ "I attract wealth because I create value."

3. The Law of Money Velocity: Wealth Loves Speed

◈ **Money moves fast—billionaires make decisions quickly and act immediately.**

Opportunities do not wait. Wealthy people **recognize trends early, invest fast, and scale quickly**.

◈ **Example:**

Elon Musk **does not wait years to launch new ideas**. He moves aggressively, which is why Tesla and SpaceX dominate their industries.

◈ **Apply This Today:**

- If you see a good investment opportunity, **act fast**.
- If you have a business idea, **launch today—perfect it later**.
- Do not overthink—**speed creates wealth**.

4. The Law of Multiplication: Billionaires Never Rely on One Income Source

◈ **The rich have multiple streams of income.** The average millionaire has **at least seven.**

Most people rely on **one job**—this is financial suicide. If you lose it, you lose everything. The wealthy **diversify income streams** so money flows from **multiple directions.**

◈ **Example:**

Warren Buffett does not **earn money from just one investment**—he owns **hundreds of companies, stocks, and assets**.

◈ **Apply This Today:**

- Start **an online business** that runs 24/7.
- Invest in **stocks, crypto, or real estate** for passive cash flow.
- Turn your skills into **digital products that sell on autopilot.**

Positioning Yourself for the Future of Wealth

We are at the beginning of a new **financial era**. The next billionaires will not be those who work harder but those who:

◈ **Leverage AI and technology** to create massive wealth.

◈ **Apply universal money laws** to attract riches effortlessly.

◈ **Take action FAST** while the world is still catching up.

Final Takeaways: Unlocking Your Quantum Wealth Potential

◈ **Start thinking like a billionaire now**—adopt an expansive wealth mindset.

◈ **Use AI and automation** to multiply income effortlessly.

◈ **Apply the hidden laws of money**—value creation, speed, and diversification.

◈ **Invest in emerging trends early**—crypto, blockchain, AI, and automation.

◈ **The future of wealth belongs to those who act now.**

Your journey to **limitless financial abundance** has just begun. ◈

Chapter 5: Taking Action – Applying the Quantum Mindset to Daily Life

You now understand the science behind success, the power of quantum wealth, the role of thoughts in shaping reality, and the future of money in the age of AI. But **knowledge alone does not create wealth—action does.**

This chapter is about **implementation**—turning everything you've learned into daily habits that will transform your financial destiny. We will also **reveal the billionaire mindset strategies** that allow the rich to **maintain and continuously grow their fortune.**

By the time you finish this chapter, you will have a **step-by-step roadmap** to apply the Quantum Mindset daily, ensuring that wealth flows into your life **effortlessly and continuously.**

The #1 Wealth Secret: The Rich Take Action Faster Than Anyone Else

Most people **think, plan, and hesitate**—billionaires **execute immediately**.

If there is **one universal truth** among the ultra-wealthy, it is this:

◈ **Speed beats perfection.**

◈ **Action beats overthinking.**

◈ **Momentum beats waiting for the right moment.**

Wealth is not about having **the perfect idea**—it's about **taking action now** and adjusting along the way. The rich do not waste time debating; they move, test, and refine.

◈ **Example:** Elon Musk did not wait until Tesla was "perfect" before launching—he **took action, adapted, and improved** as he went.

How to Apply the Quantum Mindset to Daily Life

To attract and sustain **quantum wealth**, you must build daily **rituals, habits, and decision-making frameworks** that align with the billionaire mindset.

1. Start Your Day Like a Billionaire

Your morning routine **sets the tone** for your financial success. The world's wealthiest people **prime their minds** before the day begins.

◈ **Visualization (5 min)** – See yourself already wealthy and successful.

◈ **Wealth Affirmations (2 min)** – Speak financial abundance into existence.

◈ **High-Level Learning (15 min)** – Read, listen to, or study money/AI/market trends.

◈ **Actionable Goal Setting (5 min)** – Choose **one financial action** for the day.

This routine ensures that your **first thoughts of the day are focused on abundance, opportunity, and execution.**

◈ **Example:** Oprah Winfrey and Warren Buffett start their day with **reading, mindset work, and reflection** before making decisions.

2. Operate with an Abundance Mindset (Every Decision Matters)

Your **money habits and decisions compound over time**. Every time you choose **expansion over scarcity**, you rewire your brain for wealth.

◈ **Scarcity Mindset:** "I can't afford this." → ◈ Blocks abundance
◈ **Abundance Mindset:** "How can I afford this?" → ◈ Opens creative financial solutions

◈ **Example:** Billionaires never operate from **fear-based decision-making**. Instead of focusing on **cost**, they focus on **ROI (return on investment)**.

◈ **Action Step:** Before making any decision, ask:

1. **Does this move me toward expansion or contraction?**
2. **Is this a short-term limitation or a long-term investment?**

3. The Billionaire Productivity System: Maximize Time for Wealth Creation

The rich do not **trade time for money**—they **make time work for them**.

Billionaires follow the **Pareto Principle (80/20 Rule)**:
◈ **80% of results come from 20% of actions.**
◈ They focus ONLY on **high-impact wealth activities**.

◈ **Example:**

- **Low-value tasks:** Scrolling social media, watching Netflix, doing admin work
- **High-value tasks:** Investing, networking, launching businesses, scaling income

◈ **Action Step:** Identify the **20% of actions** that generate **80% of your financial growth** and double down on them.

4. Multiple Streams of Income: How the Rich Keep Money Flowing

◈ **Secret:** No billionaire relies on ONE income source.

The wealthy **create multiple streams** of income so that money flows **continuously**.

◈ **The 7 Billionaire Income Streams:**

1. **Earned Income** – What you make from active work (job, business).
2. **Investment Income** – Money from stocks, crypto, real estate.
3. **Passive Business Income** – Income from automated businesses.
4. **Royalty & Licensing Income** – Earnings from books, music, patents.
5. **Dividend Income** – Payouts from owning shares in companies.
6. **Rental Income** – Cash flow from real estate properties.
7. **Capital Gains** – Profits from buying and selling assets.

◈ **Action Step:** Start building **at least 3 streams** of income NOW.

◈ **Example:** Mark Cuban and Jeff Bezos both **own multiple businesses, invest in startups, and generate income from various assets.**

5. Build a Powerful Network (Your Net Worth = Your Network)

Wealth is **not just about what you know—it's about WHO you know.**

Billionaires surround themselves with **other high-level thinkers**, investors, and visionaries.

◈ **Action Step:**

◈ Join **elite mastermind groups**.
◈ Connect with **wealth-conscious individuals**.
◈ Avoid **negative, scarcity-based people** who limit your growth.

◈ **Example:** Elon Musk, Larry Page, and Sergey Brin (Google founders) all **built their empires together** by forming a powerful network.

6. Invest Like a Billionaire (Make Money Work for You)

The rich do not **save money**—they **invest it so it multiplies**.

◈ **Billionaire Investment Habits:**

◈ **They invest early** – They do not wait for "perfect" market conditions.
◈ **They think long-term** – They build **generational wealth, not quick cash.**
◈ **They use leverage** – They borrow money strategically to scale wealth.

◈ **Action Step:**

- Start investing in **stocks, crypto, or real estate** today.
- Automate **monthly investments** so wealth grows over time.

◈ **Example:** Warren Buffett became a billionaire **by investing consistently over decades.**

7. Master the Art of Decision-Making

Billionaires make **faster, better decisions** than the average person.

◈ **How to Think Like a Billionaire:**

◈ **Big-picture thinking** – Focus on the next **5-10 years**, not just today.

◈ **Calculated risk-taking** – They take risks, but only when the **upside is greater than the downside**.

◈ **Speed of implementation** – They make decisions fast and adjust as needed.

◈ **Action Step:** When making a financial decision, ask:

1. **Will this create long-term wealth?**
2. **Is the upside bigger than the downside?**
3. **What is the worst-case scenario, and can I handle it?**

◈ **Example:** Richard Branson often **makes bold business moves quickly**, knowing that action creates opportunities.

Final Takeaways: Locking in the Billionaire Mindset for Life

You now have **everything you need** to think, act, and operate like the ultra-wealthy. The final step? **COMMITMENT.**

◈ **The 7 Billionaire Mindset Commandments:**

1. **Take fast action**—do not wait for "perfect conditions."
2. **Think expansively**—there are infinite ways to generate wealth.
3. **Operate in abundance, not scarcity.**
4. **Invest in multiple income streams—never rely on one source.**
5. **Network with high-level people—your circle determines your success.**
6. **Use AI and automation to scale wealth effortlessly.**
7. **Make decisions based on opportunity, not fear.**

◈ **Final Thought:** Wealth is not something you chase—it is something you **become.**

By applying the **Quantum Mindset daily**, you will enter a **state of continuous financial expansion, where wealth flows effortlessly into your life.**

◈ **Your journey to limitless financial success starts NOW.**

Appendix A: Daily Exercises to Unlock Billionaire-Level Thinking

Success is not just about working harder—it's about **thinking at a higher level** every single day. Billionaires operate on a **different mental frequency** than the average person, and their financial success is a direct result of the way they **train their minds, make decisions, and cultivate their habits.**

This appendix provides **daily exercises** designed to **rewire your brain for quantum wealth**, help you develop **unshakable financial confidence**, and ensure that you continuously operate at a **billionaire-level mindset.**

Each exercise is structured to **reprogram your subconscious**, remove **financial blocks**, and **align your mind with success and abundance.**

Section 1: Morning Power Rituals to Start the Day Like a Billionaire

The first **60 minutes** of your day determine **how the rest of your day unfolds**. Billionaires do not wake up reacting to problems—they **set powerful intentions** that align their energy with success.

Exercise 1: 5-Minute Wealth Visualization

◈ **Purpose:** To condition your brain to expect wealth and opportunity.

◈ **Instructions:**

1. **Close your eyes and take 3 deep breaths.**
2. **Visualize yourself already wealthy and successful.**
    - Imagine checking your bank account and seeing unlimited funds.
    - See yourself making powerful financial decisions.
    - Picture yourself living your dream lifestyle.
3. **Engage your emotions.** Feel the excitement, confidence, and ease of being financially limitless.

◈ **Why this works:** The **brain cannot distinguish between real and imagined experiences**. The more you visualize wealth, the more your brain **expects and attracts it**.

Exercise 2: Billionaire Wealth Affirmations

◈ **Purpose:** To rewire your subconscious with powerful money beliefs.

◈ **Instructions:** Repeat these affirmations **every morning**:

- **"I am a money magnet."**
- **"Opportunities flow to me effortlessly."**
- **"I make million-dollar decisions with confidence."**
- **"Wealth is my natural state."**
- **"Every day, I am becoming richer and more successful."**

◈ **Why this works:** Your subconscious mind **accepts whatever you repeat consistently**. Over time, these beliefs become your reality.

Exercise 3: The Billionaire Decision-Making Hack
◈ **Purpose:** To train your brain to make fast, high-impact decisions.
◈ **Instructions:**

1. **Before making any financial decision, ask yourself:**
    - **Is this an investment or an expense?**
    - **Will this help me grow my wealth long-term?**
    - **What would a billionaire do in this situation?**
2. **Decide within 60 seconds.** Avoid hesitation. Train yourself to think fast.

◈ **Why this works: Billionaires do not hesitate.** They trust their intuition and make decisions quickly.

Section 2: Midday Strategies to Strengthen Your Wealth Mindset

Most people lose focus throughout the day. These exercises **keep you in a billionaire flow state**, ensuring that every moment **moves you toward financial success.**

Exercise 4: The 80/20 Rule Focus Shift

⟐ **Purpose:** To maximize time and energy on high-impact wealth activities.

⟐ **Instructions:**

1. **List your daily activities.**
2. Identify the **20% of tasks that generate 80% of your financial success.**
    - Examples: Investing, networking, launching a business, studying market trends.
3. **Cut out low-value distractions** (social media, Netflix, useless meetings).

⟐ **Why this works:** Billionaires **only focus on high-leverage tasks** that create exponential financial growth.

Exercise 5: Money Flow Journaling

🔶 **Purpose:** To track financial expansion and remove scarcity thoughts.

🔶 **Instructions:**

1. **Write down every source of money you received today** (salary, investments, unexpected cash).
2. **List 3 new ways money can flow into your life.**
3. **Rewrite any scarcity thoughts into abundance thoughts.**
    - **Instead of:** "I don't have enough money."
    - **Write:** "Wealth is flowing to me in new and unexpected ways."

🔶 **Why this works:** What you focus on **expands**. This keeps your brain locked into wealth-building mode.

Exercise 6: The Billionaire's Midday Reset

🔶 **Purpose:** To eliminate stress and refocus on success.

🔶 **Instructions:**

1. **Take 3 deep breaths and pause all distractions.**
2. Ask yourself: **What is the ONE thing I can do right now to grow my wealth?**
3. **Do it immediately.**

🔶 **Why this works:** Small, consistent **actions create momentum**. This ensures you are **constantly moving toward financial success.**

Section 3: Nighttime Programming for Quantum Wealth Expansion

Your **subconscious mind is most receptive** just before sleep. These exercises will **lock in billionaire-level thinking while you rest.**

Exercise 7: 5-Minute Financial Gratitude Practice
◈ **Purpose:** To attract more wealth through gratitude.
◈ **Instructions:**

1. **Write down 3 things you are grateful for related to money.**
    - Example: "I am grateful for the money I received today."
2. **Express gratitude for future wealth as if it's already yours.**
    - Example: "I am so grateful for my thriving multi-million-dollar business."

◈ **Why this works: Gratitude amplifies abundance.** Billionaires constantly focus on **what they have and what's coming next.**

Exercise 8: Subconscious Money Reprogramming Before Sleep
◈ **Purpose:** To install wealth beliefs into your subconscious.
◈ **Instructions:**

1. **Listen to money affirmations** or a **binaural beats audio** while sleeping.
2. **Repeat in your mind:** "Money flows to me effortlessly" until you fall asleep.

◈ **Why this works:** Your brain **absorbs information deeply** before sleep, ensuring these beliefs **become automatic.**

Final Takeaways: Lock in the Billionaire Mindset for Life

◈ **Commit to These 8 Daily Exercises:**

◈ **Morning Visualization** – See yourself as a billionaire every day.
◈ **Wealth Affirmations** – Speak success into reality.
◈ **Fast Decision-Making Hack** – Train your brain for billionaire-level choices.
◈ **80/20 Rule Focus Shift** – Cut distractions, prioritize wealth-building.
◈ **Money Flow Journaling** – Track money growth and reprogram scarcity thoughts.
◈ **Midday Reset** – Keep momentum by taking quick action.
◈ **Financial Gratitude Practice** – Attract more money by appreciating wealth.
◈ **Subconscious Programming Before Sleep** – Let your mind absorb abundance.

◈ **Apply These for 30 Days and Watch Your Life Transform!**

- Your **mindset will be unshakable**.
- You will start to **think, act, and operate like a billionaire**.
- Financial opportunities will appear **effortlessly**.
- Money will **flow continuously** because you are **aligned with success.**

◈ **Final Thought:**
◈ **Success is not about what you do occasionally—it's about how you think daily.**

◈ **Lock in these exercises, and you will never think like an average person again.** ◈

Message from the Author:

I hope you enjoyed this book, I love astrology and knew there was not a book such as this out on the shelf. I love metaphysical items as well. Please check out my other books:

-Life of Government Benefits

-My life of Hell

-My life with Hydrocephalus

-Red Sky

-World Domination:Woman's rule

-World Domination:Woman's Rule 2: The War

-Life and Banishment of Apophis: book 1

-The Kidney Friendly Diet

-The Ultimate Hemp Cookbook

-Creating a Dispensary(legally)

-Cleanliness throughout life: the importance of showering from childhood to adulthood.

-Strong Roots: The Risks of Overcoddling children

-Hemp Horoscopes: Cosmic Insights and Earthly Healing

- Celestial Hemp Navigating the Zodiac: Through the Green Cosmos

-Astrological Hemp: Aligning The Stars with Earth's Ancient Herb

-The Astrological Guide to Hemp: Stars, Signs, and Sacred Leaves

-Green Growth: Innovative Marketing Strategies for your Hemp Products and Dispensary

-Cosmic Cannabis

-Astrological Munchies

-Henry The Hemp

-Zodiacal Roots: The Astrological Soul Of Hemp

- **Green Constellations: Intersection of Hemp and Zodiac**

-Hemp in The Houses: An astrological Adventure Through The Cannabis Galaxy

-Galactic Ganja Guide
Heavenly Hemp
Zodiac Leaves
Doctor Who Astrology
Cannastrology
Stellar Satvias and Cosmic Indicas
Celestial Cannabis: A Zodiac Journey
AstroHerbology: The Sky and The Soil: Volume 1
AstroHerbology:Celestial Cannabis:Volume 2
Cosmic Cannabis Cultivation
The Starry Guide to Herbal Harmony: Volume 1
The Starry Guide to Herbal Harmony: Cannabis Universe: Volume 2
Yugioh Astrology: Astrological Guide to Deck, Duels and more
Nightmare Mansion: Echoes of The Abyss
Nightmare Mansion 2: Legacy of Shadows
Nightmare Mansion 3: Shadows of the Forgotten
Nightmare Mansion 4: Echoes of the Damned
The Life and Banishment of Apophis: Book 2
Nightmare Mansion: Halls of Despair
Healing with Herb: Cannabis and Hydrocephalus
Planetary Pot: Aligning with Astrological Herbs: Volume 1
Fast Track to Freedom: 30 Days to Financial Independence Using AI, Assets, and Agile Hustles
Cosmic Hemp Pathways
How to Become Financially Free in 30 Days: 10,000 Paths to Prosperity
Zodiacal Herbage: Astrological Insights: Volume 1
Nightmare Mansion: Whispers in the Walls
The Daleks Invade Atlantis
Henry the hemp and Hydrocephalus

10X The Kidney Friendly Diet

Cannabis Universe: Adult coloring book

Hemp Astrology: The Healing Power of the Stars

Zodiacal Herbage: Astrological Insights: Cannabis Universe: Volume 2

Planetary Pot: Aligning with Astrological Herbs: Cannabis Universes: Volume 2

Doctor Who Meets the Replicators and SG-1: The Ultimate Battle for Survival

Nightmare Mansion: Curse of the Blood Moon

The Celestial Stoner: A Guide to the Zodiac

Cosmic Pleasures: Sex Toy Astrology for Every Sign

Hydrocephalus Astrology: Navigating the Stars and Healing Waters

Lapis and the Mischievous Chocolate Bar

Celestial Positions: Sexual Astrology for Every Sign

Apophis's Shadow Work Journal: : A Journey of Self-Discovery and Healing

Kinky Cosmos: Sexual Kink Astrology for Every Sign

Digital Cosmos: The Astrological Digimon Compendium

Stellar Seeds: The Cosmic Guide to Growing with Astrology

Apophis's Daily Gratitude Journal

Cat Astrology: Feline Mysteries of the Cosmos

The Cosmic Kama Sutra: An Astrological Guide to Sexual Positions

Unleash Your Potential: A Guided Journal Powered by AI Insights

Whispers of the Enchanted Grove

Cosmic Pleasures: An Astrological Guide to Sexual Kinks

369, 12 Manifestation Journal

Whisper of the nocturne journal(blank journal for writing or drawing)

The Boogey Book

Locked In Reflection: A Chastity Journey Through Locktober

Generating Wealth Quickly:How to Generate $100,000 in 24 Hours

Star Magic: Harness the Power of the Universe

The Flatulence Chronicles: A Fart Journal for Self-Discovery

The Doctor and The Death Moth

Seize the Day: A Personal Seizure Tracking Journal

The Ultimate Boogeyman Safari: A Journey into the Boogie World and Beyond

Whispers of Samhain: 1,000 Spells of Love, Luck, and Lunar Magic: Samhain Spell Book

Apophis's guides:Witch's Spellbook Crafting Guide for Halloween

Frost & Flame: The Enchanted Yule Grimoire of 1000 Winter Spells

The Ultimate Boogey Goo Guide & Spooky Activities for Halloween Fun

Harmony of the Scales: A Libra's Spellcraft for Balance and Beauty

The Enchanted Advent: 36 Days of Christmas Wonders

Nightmare Mansion: The Labyrinth of Screams

Harvest of Enchantment: 1,000 Spells of Gratitude, Love, and Fortune for Thanksgiving

The Boogey Chronicles: A Journal of Nightly Encounters and Shadowy Secrets

The 12 Days of Financial Freedom: A Step-by-Step Christmas Countdown to Transform Your Finances

Sigil of the Eternal Spiral Blank Journal

A Christmas Feast: Timeless Recipes for Every Meal

Holiday Stress-Free Solutions: A Survival Guide to Thriving During the Festive Season

Yu-Gi-Oh! Holiday Gifting Mastery: The Ultimate Guide for Fans and Newcomers Alike

Holiday Harmony: A Hydrocephalus Survival Guide for the Festive Season

Celestial Craft: The Witch's Almanac for 2025 – A Cosmic Guide to Manifestations, Moons, and Mystical Events

Doctor Who: The Toymaker's Winter Wonderland

Tulsa King Unveiled: A Thrilling Guide to Stallone's Mafia Masterpiece

Pendulum Craft: A Complete Guide to Crafting and Using Personalized Divination Tools

Nightmare Mansion: Santa's Eternal Eve

Starlight Noel: A Cosmic Journey through Christmas Mysteries

The Dark Architect: Unlocking the Blueprint of Existence

Surviving the Embrace: The Ultimate Guide to Encounters with The Hugging Molly

The Enchanted Codex: Secrets of the Craft for Witches, Wiccans, and Pagans

Harvest of Gratitude: A Complete Thanksgiving Guide

Yuletide Essentials: A Complete Guide to an Authentic and Magical Christmas

Celestial Smokes: A Cosmic Guide to Cigars and Astrology

Living in Balance: A Comprehensive Survival Guide to Thriving with Diabetes Insipidus

Cosmic Symbiosis: The Venom Zodiac Chronicles

The Cursed Paw of Ambition

Cosmic Symbiosis: The Astrological Venom Journal

Celestial Wonders Unfold: A Stargazer's Guide to the Cosmos (2024-2029)

The Ultimate Black Friday Prepper's Guide: Mastering Shopping Strategies and Savings

Cosmic Sales: The Astrological Guide to Black Friday Shopping

Legends of the Corn Mother and Other Harvest Myths

Whispers of the Harvest: The Corn Mother's Journal

The Evergreen Spellbook

The Doctor Meets the Boogeyman

The White Witch of Rose Hall's SpellBook

The Gingerbread Golem's Shadow: A Study in Sweet Darkness

The Gingerbread Golem Codex: An Academic Exploration of Sweet Myths

The Gingerbread Golem Grimoire: Sweet Magicks and Spells for the Festive Witch

The Curse of the Gingerbread Golem

10-minute Christmas Crafts for kids

Christmas Crisis Solutions: The Ultimate Last-Minute Survival Guide

Gingerbread Golem Recipes: Holiday Treats with a Magical Twist

The Infinite Key: Unlocking Mystical Secrets of the Ages

Enchanted Yule: A Wiccan and Pagan Guide to a Magical and Memorable Season

Dinosaurs of Power: Unlocking Ancient Magick

Astro-Dinos: The Cosmic Guide to Prehistoric Wisdom

Gallifrey's Yule Logs: A Festive Doctor Who Cookbook

The Dino Grimoire: Secrets of Prehistoric Magick

The Gift They Never Knew They Needed

The Gingerbread Golem's Culinary Alchemy: Enchanting Recipes for a Sweetly Dark Feast

A Time Lord Christmas: Holiday Adventures with the Doctor

Krampusproofing Your Home: Defensive Strategies for Yule

Silent Frights: A Collection of Christmas Creepypastas to Chill Your Bones

Santa Raptor's Jolly Carnage: A Dino-Claus Christmas Tale

Prehistoric Palettes: A Dino Wicca Coloring Journey

The Christmas Wishkeeper Chronicles

The Starlight Sleigh: A Holiday Journey

Elf Secrets: The True Magic of the North Pole

Candy Cane Conjurations

Cooking with Kids: Recipes Under 20 Minutes

Doctor Who: The TARDIS Confiscation

The Anxiety First Aid Kit: Quick Tools to Calm Your Mind

Frosty Whispers: A Winter's Tale

The Infinite Key: Unlocking the Secrets to Prosperity, Resilience, and Purpose

The Grasping Void: Why You'll Regret This Purchase

Astrology for Busy Bees: Star Signs Simplified

The Instant Focus Formula: Cut Through the Noise

The Secret Language of Colors: Unlocking the Emotional Codes

Sacred Fossil Chronicles: Blank Journal

The Christmas Cottage Miracle

Feeding Frenzy: Graboid-Inspired Recipes

Manifest in Minutes: The Quick Law of Attraction Guide

The Symbiote Chronicles: Doctor Who's Venomous Journey

Think Tiny, Grow Big: The Minimalist Mindset

The Energy Key: Unlocking Limitless Motivation

New Year, New Magic: Manifesting Your Best Year Yet

Unstoppable You: Mastering Confidence in Minutes

Infinite Energy: The Secret to Never Feeling Drained

Lightning Focus: Mastering the Art of Productivity in a Distracted World

Saturnalia Manifestation Magick: A Guide to Unlocking Abundance During the Solstice

Graboids and Garland: The Ultimate Tremors-Themed Christmas Guide

12 Nights of Holiday Magic

The Power of Pause: 60-Second Mindfulness Practices

The Quick Reset: How to Reclaim Your Life After Burnout

The Shadow Eater: A Tale of Despair and Survival

The Micro-Mastery Method: Transform Your Skills in Just Minutes a Day

Reclaiming Time: How to Live More by Doing Less
Chronovore: The Eternal Nexus
The Mind Reset: Unlocking Your Inner Peace in a Chaotic World
Confidence Code: Building Unshakable Self-Belief
Baby the Vampire Terrier
Baby the Vampire Terrier's Christmas Adventure
Celestial Streams: The Content Creator's Astrology Manual
The Wealth Whisperer: Unlocking Abundance with Everyday Actions
The Energy Equation: Maximize Your Output Without Burning Out
The Happiness Algorithm: Science-Backed Steps to Joyful Living
Stress-Free Success: Achieving Goals Without Anxiety
Mindful Wealth: The New Blueprint for Financial Freedom
The Festive Flavors of New Year: A Culinary Celebration
The Master's Gambit: Keys of Eternal Power
Shadowed Secrets: Groundhog Day Mysteries
Beneath the Burrow: Lessons from the Groundhog
Spring's Whispers: The Groundhog's Prediction
The Limitless Mindset: Unlock Your Untapped Potential
The Focus Funnel: How to Cut Through Chaos and Get Results
Bold Moves: Building Courage to Live on Your Terms
The Daily Shift: Simple Practices for Lasting Transformation
The Quarter-Life Reset: Thriving in Your 20s and 30s
The Art of Shadowplay: Building Your Own Personal Myth
The Eternal Loop: Finding Purpose in Repetition
Burrowing Wisdom: Life Lessons from the Groundhog
Shadow Work: A Groundhog Day Perspective
Love in Bloom: 5-Minute Romantic Gestures
The Shadowspell Codex: Secrets of Forbidden Magick
The Burnout Cure: Finding Balance in a Busy World
The Groundhog Prophecy: Unlocking Seasonal Secrets
Nog Tales: The Spirited History of Eggnog

Six More Weeks: Embracing Seasonal Transitions
The Lumivian Chronicles: Fragments of the Fifth Dimension
Money on Your Mind: A Beginner's Guide to Wealth
The Focus Fix: Breaking Through Distraction
January's Spirit Keepers: Mystical Protectors of the Cold
Creativity Unchained: Unlocking Your Wildest Ideas in 2025
Manifestation Mastery: 365 Days to Rewrite Your Reality
The Groundhog's Mirror: Reflecting on Change
The Weeping Angels' Christmas Curse
Burrowed in Time: A Groundhog Day Journey
Heartbeats: Poems to Share with Your Valentine
Dino Wicca: The Sacred Grimoire of Prehistoric Magick
Courage of the Pride: Finding Your Inner Roar
The Lion's Leap: Bold Moves for Big Results
Healthy Hustle: Achieving Without Overworking
Practical Manifesting: Turning Dreams into Reality in 2025
Jurassic Pharaohs: Unlocking the Magick of Ancient Egypt and Dino Wicca
The Happiness Equation: Small Changes for Big Joy
The Confidence Compass: Finding Your Inner Strength
Whispers in the Hollow: Tales of the Forgotten Beasts
Echoes from the Hollow: The Return of Forgotten Beasts
The Hollow Ascendant: The Rise of the Forgotten Beasts
The Relationship Reset: Building Better Connections
Mastering the Morning: How to Win the Day Before 8 AM
The Shadow's Dance: Groundhog Day Symbolism
Cupid's Kitchen: Quick Valentine's Day Recipes
Valentine's Day on a Budget: Love Without Breaking the Bank
Astrocraft: Aligning the Stars in the World of Minecraft
Forecasting Life: Groundhog Day Reflections
Bleeding Hearts: Twisted Tales of Valentine's Terror
Herbal Smoke Revolution: The Ultimate Guide to Nature's Cigarette Alternative

Winter's Wrath: The Complete Survival Blueprint for Extreme Freezes.

The Groundhog's Shadow: A Tale of Seasons

Burrowed Insights: Wisdom from the Groundhog

Sensual Strings: The Art of Erotic Bondage

Whispered Flames: Unlocking the Power of Fire Play

Forgotten Shadows: A Guide to Cryptids Lost to Time

Six Weeks of Secrets: Groundhog Day's Hidden Messages

Shadows and Cycles: Groundhog Day Reflections

The Art of Love Letters: Crafting the Perfect Message

Romantic Getaways at Home: Turning Your Space into Paradise

Purrfect Brews: A Cat Lover's Guide to Coffee and Companionship

The Groundhog's Wisdom: Timeless Lessons for Modern Life

The Shadow Oracle: Groundhog Day as a Predictor

Emerging from the Burrow: A Journey of Renewal

The Language of Love: Learning Your Partner's Love Style

Authorpreneur: The Ultimate Blueprint for Writing, Publishing, and Thriving as an Author

Weathering the Seasons: Groundhog Day Perspectives

Valentine's Day Magic: A Guide to Romantic Rituals

The Shadow Chronicles: Stories of Groundhog Day

Love and Laughter: Fun Games for Valentine's Day

AstroRealty: Unlocking the Stars for Property Success

The Groundhog's Path: A Guide to Seasonal Balance

Groundhog Day Diaries: Reflections in the Shadow

The Groundhog's Light: Illuminating the Path Ahead

Valentine's Traditions from Around the World

AI Wealth Revolution: Unlocking the Trillionaire Mindset

Love Rekindled: Reigniting Passion in Relationships

Single and Thriving: Self-Love on Valentine's Day

Emerald Legends: Mystical Tales of Ireland

Green Alchemy: Harnessing Nature's Magic
The Hearts of Horror: A Valentine's Day Nightmare
The Leprechaun's Guide to Wealth and Wisdom
Dancing with the Sidhe: Celebrating the Otherworld
Shamrocks and Shadows: Mysteries of the Green Isle
Emerald Energy: Harnessing Luck and Growth
The Gingerbread Golem's Valentine: A Sweetheart's Guide to Love and Enchantment
The Celtic Knot: Weaving Life and Destiny
Green Fire: Elemental Magic for St. Patrick's Day
Clover Chronicles: Finding Your Inner Luck
Ireland's Mystical Creatures: A Field Guide
Gingerbread Golem's Love Almanac
Prowl and Thrive: The Lion's Guide to Success
Love Alchemy: Transforming Your Life Through Heart Energy
WORLD DOMINATION: Woman's Rule 3:The New Life
The Midnight Rose: A Guide to Lunar Love Spells
The Forbidden Letters: Writing Your Own Love Prophecy
Luck and Lore: St. Patrick's Day for Modern Mystics
The Green Path: A Pagan Celebration of Renewal
The Dark Architect's Guide to Reprogramming Reality
Prankster's Paradise: A Guide to Harmless Hijinks
Manifest Your Reality: The Law of Attraction Simplified
The TARDIS Owner's Manual: Understanding the Doctor's Ship: *A complete guide to the TARDIS, its technology, secrets, and mysteries*
Starlit Romance: Astrology Secrets for Finding True Love
The Time Lord's Atlas: A Complete Guide to the Whoniverse: ***A breakdown of the locations, planets, and dimensions explored in Doctor Who***
Sweetheart Shadows: The Dark Side of Love and Attraction
February Fire: Reigniting Passion in Every Area of Life

The Self-Love Toolkit: 5 Ways to Embrace Who You Are
February Sparks: Ignite Your Dreams in 28 Days
March to Success: A 31-Day Action Blueprint
Ancient Paths: The 13 Sacred Principles of Dino Wicca
Echoes of Tomorrow: Navigating the AI Revolution
The Wellness Blueprint: Balancing Mind, Body, and Soul
Green Horizons: Sustainable Living for a Better Tomorrow
The AI Wealth Code: How to Make Millions with Automation
AI-Powered Creativity: Writing, Art, and Music for Profit
Extinction Rites: Rebirthing Your Soul Through Prehistoric Magick
Sacred Serpents tarot
Celestial Enchantment blank journal
Star Strains
Culinary Journeys: Exploring Global Flavors at Home
The Hollowvale Curse
The Hollowvale Harvest
The Egg of Transformation: Awakening Your Inner Power
Blooming Into Power: A Wiccan Guide to Spring Awakening
The Nightmare Nexus: The Third Doctor's Perilous Haunting
Digital Detox: Reclaiming Your Life in a Connected World
Ostara's Path: Walking the Spiral of Renewal
The Sacred Hare
Financial Freedom: Building Wealth in the Modern Age
Spring's Cauldron: Stirring the Waters of Change
The Hollowvale Pact
Quantum Consciousness: The Science of Reality Shifting
The Hollowvale Hunger
The Sacred Waters Within: A Witch's Guide to Hydrocephalus Magick
The Raven's Nest: Building a Life of Unshakable Stability
AI and the Human Mind: The Future of Intelligence
The Hollowvale Reckoning

Timeless Love: Building and Maintaining Lasting Relationships

The Raven's Roar: Unlocking Unstoppable Confidence

Raven Sight: Awakening Intuition and Inner Wisdom

The Butterfly Effect: Small Changes, Big Transformations

Taming the Boogeyman: How to Conquer Your Inner Fears

The Magick of Green: Awakening Earth's Energy in You

The Entrepreneurial Mindset: Secrets to Business Success

The Hollowvale End

The Shadow Luck Ritual: Reclaiming Power from Your Dark Side

Spring Magick for Beginners: A Simple Guide to Seasonal Energy Work

Doctor Who: The Hollowvale Conundrum

The March of Miracles: Unlocking Synchronicities in Spring

Unveiling the Cosmos: A Guide to Stargazing and Space Exploration

The Ultimate Guide to Surviving an Economic Collapse

The AI Gold Rush: How to Profit from the AI Revolution

Bastet's Shadow: The Hidden Power of Feline Magick

The Bastet Codex: Unlocking the Goddess's Magickal Secrets

Purring Spells: Harnessing Bastet's Healing Frequencies

Bastet's Nine Lives: Rebirth, Transformation, and Immortality Spells

Primal Currents: Hydrocephalus Magick in the Path of Dino Wicca

The Digital Gold Rush: Mastering E-Commerce and Online Sales

Future Shock: Adapting to the Next Decade of Change

If you want solar for your home go here: https://www.harborsolar.live/apophisenterprises/

Get Some Tarot cards: https://www.makeplayingcards.com/sell/apophis-occult-shop

<u>**Get some shirts: https://www.bonfire.com/store/apophis-shirt-emporium/**</u>

Instagrams:
@apophis_enterprises,
@apophisbookemporium,
@apophisscardshop
Twitter: @apophisenterpr1
Tiktok:@apophisenterprise
Youtube: @sg1fan23477, @FiresideRetreatKingdom
Hive: @sg1fan23477
CheeLee: @SG1fan23477

Podcast: Apophis Chat Zone: https://open.spotify.com/show/5zXbrCLEV2xzCp8ybrfHsk?si=fb4d4fdbdce44dec

Newsletter: https://apophiss-newsletter-27c897.beehiiv.com/

If you want to support me or see posts of other projects that I have come over to: **buymeacoffee.com/mpetchinskg**

I post there daily several times a day

Get your Dinowicca or Christmas themed digital products, especially Santa Raptor songs and other musics. Here: **https://sg1fan23477.gumroad.com**

Apophis Yuletide Digital has not only digital Christmas items, but it will have all things with Dinowicca as well as other Digital products.

www.ingramcontent.com/pod-product-compliance
Lightning Source LLC
LaVergne TN
LVHW022027200926
848481LV00007B/2579